Schools Under Siege

Guns, Gangs, and Hidden Dangers

Carl Bosch

—Issues in Focus—

Enslow Publishers, Inc.

44 Fadem Road   PO Box 38
Box 699   Aldershot
Springfield, NJ 07081   Hants GU12 6BP
USA   UK

Library of Congress Cataloging-in-Publication Data

Bosch, Carl W.
    Schools under siege: guns, gangs, and hidden dangers / by Carl Bosch.
       p. cm. — (Issues in Focus)
    Includes bibliographical references and index.
    Summary: Explores the issues surrounding the growing problem of violence in
schools, in both rural and urban areas.
    ISBN 0-89490-908-8
    1. Schools—United States—Safety measures—Juvenile literature. 2. School
violence—United States—Prevention—Juvenile literature. [1. School violence.
2. Violence.] I. Title. II. Series: Issues in focus (Hillside, N.J.)
LB2864.5.B67 1997
363.119371—DC20   96-36363
                                     CIP
                                     AC

Printed in the United States of America

10 9 8 7 6 5 4 3 2 1

Illustration Credits: Keith Olsen, pp. 9, 23, 46, 55, 59, 87, 94; Library of
Congress, pp. 30, 38, 67, 80, 99; The White House, Office of Photography,
p. 75.

Cover Illustrations: AP/Wide World Photos; Enslow Publishers, Inc.

Contents

1

School Violence

Students are dying in American schools. They are mugged, harassed, abused, and threatened daily. Eight-year-olds are afraid their lunch money will be stolen. Teenagers keep a watch out for the next drive-by shooting. Young people boast of violent actions. Drug use and sales are rampant. Gangs rule the corridors. Weapons are everywhere. Teachers are scared. Classrooms are tension-filled. Administrators are forced into running schools that resemble prisons.

About 3 million violent crimes and thefts occur at schools every year. Since 1985, almost one million youths between the ages of twelve and nineteen have been victims of violent crime each year.[1] Richard Riley, education secretary in the Clinton administration, stated that an estimated one out of every five high school students carries a gun, knife, or club on a regular basis.[2] From 1991 to 1994, Detroit-area school officials confiscated an

> In a Washington, D.C., junior high school, youths fearful of the effect of guns and gangs plan their own funerals in case they should die.[3]

assortment of weapons. The weapons included: a .357 magnum, a 9mm Glock assault weapon, an Uzi machine gun, and an assortment of knives, stun guns, BB guns, brass knuckles, martial arts weapons, darts, clubs, explosives, Mace, pepper gas, and metal pipes.[4]

Violence in schools affects teachers and students. It is brought into classrooms because it exists in society, in the home, and in entertainment. Schools cannot shut their doors and expect a safe "castle" where outside influences don't enter. Teresa Zutter, the education director of the Fairfax County (Virginia) Juvenile Detention Center states:

> There's almost a sense that everything is out of their control. Many of the children come in harder than they were 10 years ago. The layers you have to cut through to reach them are thicker. And getting there takes longer and more perseverance than ever before. They're afraid they're going to fall apart so they armor themselves.[5]

Youngsters who live in violence carry it into school.

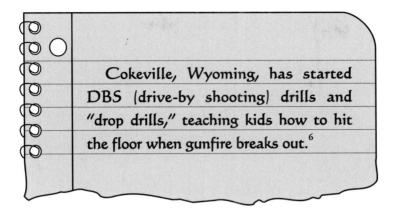

Cokeville, Wyoming, has started DBS (drive-by shooting) drills and "drop drills," teaching kids how to hit the floor when gunfire breaks out.[6]

This rise in school crime and violence is not limited to the largest cities or the most difficult neighborhoods. Small towns have their share of problems. The far-reaching effect of violence and crime extends to all corners of America.

In the past, students resolved difficulties with arguments and fistfights. At the worst, a knife or a zip gun (a gun made at home from hardware store parts) might have been used. Schools were known and supported by parents and neighbors as a safe haven. Violence and fights were not tolerated. Problem students were quickly expelled or often dropped out. Young people did not bring their problems into school. Such difficulties were handled in the neighborhood or on the street. Fear of school authorities, combined with family pride and respect for the institution of school, promoted a climate generally free of major conflicts.

The halls of many schools are filled with anger, revenge, sarcasm, and conflict. Rumors and threats are carried from student to student. The cafeteria can be a

> "A girl assaulted my sister in the cafeteria. They both got thrown out of school for three days. If it was real serious, they wouldn't be allowed back for a week."
> —fourteen-year-old girl, Baltimore.[7]

room filled with tension and aggression. Many students see others fighting and are disturbed. Sometimes the violence is directed toward teachers. School is no longer a safe place where young people can concentrate and focus on learning. School for many youngsters has been transformed into an aggressive and fearful place to spend time. Those schools situated in or near large urban centers may suffer the most from violence, but statistics from all fifty states and Canada show that disciplinary problems and crime are on the rise.

Every day fifteen children between the ages of fourteen and nineteen are killed by guns. One hundred thirty-five thousand students bring weapons to school each day. One hundred sixty thousand students stay home every day because they are afraid to go to school. One out of eleven teachers has been attacked in school.

Every year in the United States, approximately one hundred thousand students carry guns to school.

Twenty-nine percent of teachers have thought of leaving the profession because of school violence.

A Metropolitan Life survey completed in 1994 highlights the fears and problems.[8] One fifth of students fear they will be assaulted. Thirteen percent reported carrying weapons to school. One fourth of teachers fear assault inside or near their schools.

There are many reasons why violence has come to live in schools across the United States. American society has changed dramatically in the last thirty years. One of the most negative changes involves the increase in drug use and crime. Drug abuse from cocaine and crack to marijuana and heroin destroys lives, families, and neighborhoods. Users and dealers are in the schools. Money is made from drug trafficking. Gang members often take over the drug trade and gang influence filters drug sales into schools.

> Despite reports of gang involvement in drug trafficking, researchers have found that street gang structures do not organizationally support drug distribution, but drug-selling cliques within the gang may operate. That is, individual gang members may be involved in distribution networks, but in most instances these networks are not organized gang activities.[9]

The entertainment industry also promotes violence. Gangsta rap songs talk about killing police and mistreating girls and women. Movies aim for the highest allowable level of violence to attract large audiences. Youngsters are easily allowed in at R-rated films. Television has pushed the censorship code to the edge.

Stories and words on sitcoms that would never have been allowed twenty years ago are now commonplace. Violence on network dramas is excessive.

Incidents of child abuse are growing. More parents turn to violence toward their children as a type of discipline. Newspapers stories headline the latest tales of a preschooler being abandoned or abused. Social service agencies are overworked and understaffed. Agencies seldom take a child away from a family unless there is severe and obvious abuse. School counselors and social workers often deal with physically and emotionally abused children.

Many children do not have the foundation of a loving, caring family. Angry divorces result in children growing up in aggressive and violent homes. Youngsters who are raised in such homes may turn out to be just as aggressive as their parents. They are mistrustful, guarded, angry, and defensive.

Formerly viewed as role models, celebrities can no longer be looked to as examples of outstanding citizens.

In Greenwich High School in Connecticut, several white senior boys left a coded message in their yearbook that was violently anti-black and racist.

11

Many movie stars, athletes, and other celebrities break the law and flaunt the rules of society. Professional athletes swear in post-game interviews and young people think it is cool. Actors and musicians are convicted on assault charges and teens still flock to their movies and concerts. As long as a celebrity is rich and on television young people want to be like that individual.

Racism and interracial tension are not better than in the past. In many regards racial conflict is actually worse. Busing failed to help schools integrate in a positive way. Large cities, where many minority students live, have less money to put into school programs. Many minority students feel cheated by the educational and social system.

The attitude of society is mirrored in the school classroom, hallway, and activities as well. If aggression and fighting exist in a neighborhood, they will find their way into school. The school has become a pressure cooker of activities unrelated to education. Crimes are committed in schools when outsiders and adults come into the school looking for individuals to settle a score.

A thirteen-year-old girl slashed a thirteen-year-old boy in the face with a razor as they fought over a sweat jacket in the corridor of a junior high school in Brooklyn, New York.[10]

Violence in New York State's public schools as reported by superintendents in 1993 sounds like a list of battle statistics:[11]	
Disorderly conduct:	more than 24,000 incidents
Harassment:	more than 19,500 incidents
Assault:	more than 8,800 incidents
Vandalism:	more than 6,800 incidents
Larceny:	more than 5,500 incidents
Menacing:	more than 5,400 incidents
Weapon possession:	more than 3,100 incidents
Reckless endangerment:	more than 3,100 incidents

Beatings and shootings result and innocent bystanders are harmed. Gunshots fired in conflicts hit school buses. One measure of the degree to which society has invaded school is that personal beepers go off in school classrooms to alert students that their drug dealer has arrived. A safe campus is a myth.

Most young people who bring weapons to school do so out of fear. Students are afraid that without a weapon for defense they will be left at the mercy of other students who are "carrying." They believe that walking down the hallway of a school can be dangerous. In order to protect themselves students feel they must give the impression of being strong and powerful. They will fight back if provoked. Attitudes, pants, clothing styles, facial hair, slang, and profanity all add to an appearance of being tough, uncaring, and unapproachable. School for many youngsters is a place to be constantly on guard and ready for anything. Carrying a gun for some students comes with the territory. Unfortunately, if a youngster has a gun in school, it may be used.

There were approximately 87,000 violent incidents involving 107,000 students in the 1993 school year in New York State.[12] In the 1993–94 school year in New York City alone, 3,095 weapons (including handguns, rifles, knives, and box cutters) were seized in school. An additional 3,349 weapons were confiscated through the schools' metal detectors. The school chancellor at that time, Ramon Cortines, believed the huge increase in the number of weapons seized was due to improved reporting by school authorities. He felt school principals in the past often underreported the amount of school crime in

In Wayne County, Michigan, a seventh grader brought a pellet gun that resembled a .357 magnum to school. He pointed it at the school bus driver's head and pulled the trigger.[13]

> Des Moines, Iowa, has reported more incidences of school violence in 1994 than at any time in the past. Guns have been fired near school buildings. A student was accused of threatening another student with a broken bottle. A teacher has been slapped and another has been hit in the face with a piece of concrete.[14]

an effort to salvage school reputations. Cortines stated: "These are not school issues, these are community issues. These statistics are not an indictment of young people or schools, it's an indictment of our society."[15]

Crime and violence in schools is found everywhere. School districts of all sizes report a general increase in all categories of violent school-based behavior. Many adults believe the problem is centered in New York, Detroit, Chicago, Dallas, Washington, St. Louis, or Los Angeles and not in their own towns. That type of thinking permits millions of students to attend school in fear each year. Violence existing in large city schools today is found on a smaller scale in numerous villages and townships. It exists in rural America and is moving into earlier grades each year.

Repeated from state to state, the tide of violence in

our schools is rising dramatically. The violence has grown more aggressive and damaging. Fighting with fists grew to involve bats, knives, chains, and ultimately guns. Once firearms entered the schools all students were at immediate risk. Fights hurt innocent bystanders as well as the people fighting. Now, when a gun is involved, any individual in the school building can be hurt or even killed. The safety factor for all students disappears.

Health and Emotional Concerns

If schools should be safe, they should also be healthy. They should be buildings students can attend confidently, knowing they are safe from violence and that their health and physical safety are also important. The rooms, corridors, playgrounds, and cafeterias should pose no health concerns.

Sometimes the physical condition of the school building is a threat to students. Many schools are "sick" buildings. They are unsafe places for both students and teachers. *Sick school syndrome* is the term used to describe a school building that is generally unhealthy. Sometimes the physical condition of the school building is a threat to students. Students cannot learn in an unhealthy, distracting environment.

Many American schools were built before World War II. Being over fifty years old, they are wearing out. In some large cities, school buildings are literally crumbling apart. Paint is chipping off walls, cracked or broken windows remain that way for months, and antiquated heating systems blast heat to some rooms while others freeze. Walls are covered with graffiti.

Bathrooms are partially out of order or so old and lacking in privacy that students simply refuse to use them. In many places city or county budgets are inadequate for needed repairs.

In an Alabama elementary school a ceiling collapsed just forty minutes after classes were dismissed. In a Chicago elementary school, students wear winter coats all day long to ward off cold air blowing through holes in the roof and windows. Some District of Columbia schools have been closed due to chronic fire code violations.[16]

We now know that the asbestos used to safeguard schools from fires in the 1950s and 1960s can cause cancer. Watching asbestos-removal experts working in a school—equipped with "astronaut-type" gear, breathing equipment, and specialized tools—can be frightening. That asbestos might have damaged the health of students and teachers who worked, studied, and learned in those areas. Allergy-aggravating conditions—dust, mold, dirt, bacteria, and insects—plague many older schools. A school cannot be safe unless it is healthy.

Many schools are not safe. Ranging from physical violence and crime to unhealthy buildings, they are not positive places for children, adolescents, and young adults. This book will explain the reasons why schools are not safe. It will also show how schools are coping with the problem and what you can do to make yourself and your school safe.

2

Reasons for Fear

American society has changed and so have American schools. The differences in three short decades are dramatic. Complex social problems have affected schools negatively. Drug abuse, media violence, families in crisis, poverty, racism, urban decay, widespread availability of handguns, loss of respect, and mainstreaming of disruptive students all have taken their toll. These difficult challenges create the situation that exists in schools today. When added together they make a sad statement of violence and fear that resounds through many school hallways.

Rise of Drug Addiction and Alcohol Use

Many studies report that drug abuse is on the rise again after dropping during the late 1980s. This new upward trend is disappointing. Marijuana and cocaine today are more powerful than their counterparts were twenty years ago. New, highly addictive drugs like crack are easily available. The University of Michigan's Institute for Social Research surveyed about fifty thousand students and found that "over a third of all eighth-graders have used some illicit drug, including inhalants, while over 40 percent of 10th graders and nearly 50 percent of all 12th graders have done so."[1] The report also states that among eighth graders, 13 percent experimented with marijuana in 1993, about twice the level of experimentation three years earlier. This is a sharp increase. Constant media messages in the past regarding the dangers of drugs had helped to diminish drug use. In recent years media attention to the problem has decreased. Now student fear of drug use is diminishing.

Crime and drug abuse go hand in hand. Street dealing, cutting drugs into smaller quantities for sale, and selling drugs to young people are all growing in demand. Dealing drugs is a quick and easy way to make money. Drug dealing lends itself to violence and efforts to control neighborhood turf—including schools—for the sale of drugs.

Young people who are addicted to drugs display extreme behavior. Drugs are expensive. Theft, harassment, and burglary are committed by young people with drug dependencies. Victims include parents, neighbors, and schoolmates. The messages of school—hard work, delayed rewards, and finding value in achievement—are forgotten in a haze of drug use.

Many students come to school having taken drugs. A student who is high on drugs is unprepared to do schoolwork. The school environment is weakened by the presence of students involved with drugs. Education and its demands and requirements are unimportant to many middle school and high school students who are involved with drugs and alcohol. Also, abusers lack the attention span and concentration needed for learning.

Teenage drug dealers often make their sales and connections at school. While in school, some students are more concerned with buying drugs than with learning. Many schools have forbidden students to carry beepers. The beepers are often used to contact drug dealers. Students skip school to buy drugs, or hide out in bathrooms and get high between classes.

Alcohol is the drug of choice for many students. Drinking in American society is more socially acceptable than using drugs. Adults drink and the popular media advertises alcohol. Young people want to "party" as well. Many athletic team members who frown on marijuana and cocaine think it is fine to "get a buzz" on the weekend with alcohol. Monday morning stories are filled with, "I was so drunk on Saturday night!" Many high school students' parties, closely connected with after-school activities like sports events or dances, are not considered cool by young people unless drugs or alcohol are available. Parents even condone drinking by underage students by taking car keys away at parties. Their attitude helps foster a drinking mentality. "They're going to drink anyway, so I'd rather have them do it here and not drink and drive."

Drugs are more prevalent, stronger, and more dangerous than ever before. They are present in the lives of many teenagers and are found being passed, bought, sold, and shared in and around schools. Drug use has a direct and negative effect on motivation, achievement, grades, and schools.

Violence and Conflicting Messages Through the Media

All forms of media have pushed the limits of social acceptability over the last two decades. Television programs have become more daring and suggestive both in language and in the content of their story lines. Parental warnings are issued more and more frequently before the broadcast of made-for-TV movies. Shows popular with teenagers, like *Beverly Hills, 90210* and *Melrose Place,* often deal with adult or controversial themes. Many young students rush home after school to catch the latest episode of their favorite, increasingly risqué soap opera.

Some popular music artists such as Madonna have pushed sexuality into the forefront of their music and concerts. Certain rap artists, especially those performing gangsta rap, express defiance of widely accepted standards of behavior. The words to some rap songs promote disrespect and violence toward women and encourage violence toward police and authority figures. Parental warning labels are now used to alert parents to the content on CDs and tapes. Television music channels such as MTV have established the fame and fortune of many rock groups who sometimes focus on disturbing and violent scenes within their videos. Heavy-metal groups focus on violence and satanism. A group called Nine Inch Nails displays MTV videos with images that are sadistic and disturbing.

Despite this expansion of overt sex and negative attitudes into the mass media, many parents are not aware of what their children listen to or watch. Many parents have never heard a single song by an artist or group that their children listen to frequently. This is partly because so many teenagers listen to music through headphones, so no one else hears. Young people can quote the lyrics to songs that are more violent and horrifying than any X-rated film. Teenagers state that music does not influence the way they act. Most research has found, however, that although students may not be more violent they are definitely desensitized to violence. They need larger and louder thrills to be moved or excited. They are not affected by the suffering of others. They see the world in simplistic terms. Violence and aggression impress them as reasonable reactions to difficulties.

Popular movies add to this climate of violence. Many young people regularly watch movies rated PG-13 and R, some containing violence or horror. Popular films attempt to be louder, angrier, and more aggressive and have a larger body count to attract a wide audience, especially among the sought after sixteen-to-thirty-year-old age group. Sometimes a film has a dramatic effect on people's lives. *The Program*, a film about high school football teams, had a tragic influence. In the original version of the movie, teenage football players would lie along the white line in the middle of the road at night as cars passed by, to test their courage. In real life several students performed the same deed, only to be struck and killed by passing cars.

Psychologists and child experts claim that, similar to the effect of some music, a general desensitization has taken place in American culture due to television and film. Children watching many hours of television see thousands

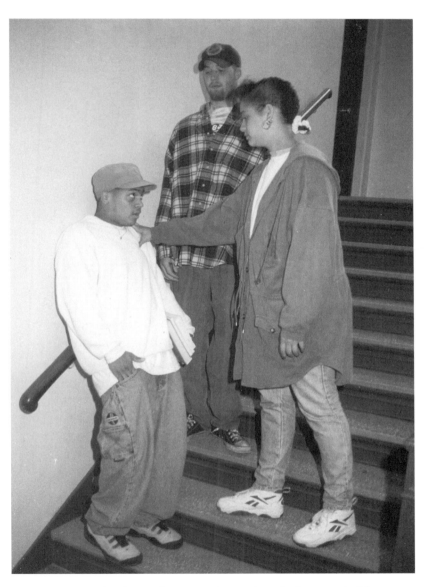

In many schools, students are harassed and threatened. These incidents often end in violence.

of acts of violence and murder by the time they are twelve years old. Just as television is very persuasive in selling automobiles, cereals, and clothing, it is powerful in selling images of violence. Cartoons are filled with explosions, gunfire, fighting, and aggression. In some preschool and nursery school programs throughout the country, young children are no longer allowed to wear or carry *Mighty Morphin Power Ranger* shirts, hats, and book bags. Youngsters were imitating their karate heroes with constant chops and kicks that were dangerous to other children. Teachers are attempting to curb this type of "playing."

The debate rages as to whether movies and television mirror what society desires or whether the film industry helps to create the need among moviegoers and television watchers. In May 1995, Robert Dole, then a U.S. senator, made an accusatory speech blaming the movie industry for helping to diminish the moral level of American families. Many religious and political leaders supported Dole's statements. But many entertainment industry representatives and even some government officials disagreed with Dole's conclusion that entertainment is responsible for social values.

A sixth grader in Des Moines, Iowa, brought a pipe bomb to his elementary school in 1994.[2]

While that debate rages, there is a need to continue to explore whether the violence in the media does in fact affect young people and their attitude in school. Does the fast-paced level of television and its commercials allow appropriate school behavior? Can teachers expect effort and calm attention from students who are used to being stimulated by the energetic images they see on television? How can schools attempt to increase reading skills in a population that would rather be entertained by film and video than engage in the quiet activity of reading? Does media violence play a part in school behavior?

Families in Crisis or Transition

The American family is under severe stress as the country approaches the twenty-first century. Referrals to state and federal agencies for neglect and abuse are on the rise. Social workers have a difficult time managing the sheer volume of cases. Abuse cases take priority over "mere" neglect. Abandoned and abused children have difficulty coping with all aspects of life.

Divorce is a common occurrence, passing the 50 percent mark for all marriages. The pressures of raising children, maintaining a home, and being positive role models are too difficult for many adults. Families break apart for a variety of reasons. Angry divorces find children splitting their time shuttling between two parents. Contradictory messages and blaming occur.

Children can mirror the difficulties in their home. They often imitate what they see around them. Divorce can be ugly and angry. Many families self-destruct into name-calling and accusation. Children who observe or are

> The incidence of reported child abuse tripled between 1976 and 1986.[3] It reached more than 2.7 million cases in 1992.[4]

part of such difficult home settings take some of that anger into themselves and are damaged by the experience. When home and family, the most basic relationships and institutions in life, are not only upsetting but hurtful, children cannot be expected to trust in or care about others. If those adults who should be caring act angry and vindictive, children learn to be that way as well.[5]

Many young people are not able to shut off the experiences of home and walk into school leaving family troubles behind. They bring their emotional problems with them. Schools are forced to deal with those emotions as they are played out in classrooms. These students may be distracted, uncaring, or disinterested. They are not motivated to focus on school. Some become bullies and treat others cruelly. Some act out in violent ways, aggressively confronting teachers and other students. School counselors and psychologists spend time offering support and attempting to help. Their efforts are aimed at helping students to cope with the demands and difficulties of life at home and at school.

Poverty

Of all the poor in the United States, 40 percent are children. Perhaps surprisingly, less than 9 percent of the poor in the United States live in our nation's largest cities. Most live in rural areas, small towns, and small metropolitan areas. Twenty-five percent of all homeless people are children.

Students who live in poverty are not physically or emotionally equipped to learn in school. These children suffer from poor nutrition, substandard living conditions, lack of stimulation, and poor health. Children trapped in poverty are absent from school at a much higher rate than those from more affluent school districts. Immunization among nonwhite children is less that half of the immunization levels of most western European nations. This means minority children are more likely to get sick. They may miss more days of school, making it hard to catch up on learning. Poor students are less able to use school and the education system to make a better life for themselves. The pressure to leave school and get a job is often too great.

Poverty may be a reason why young people turn to

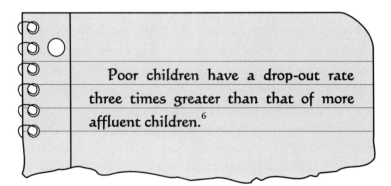

Poor children have a drop-out rate three times greater than that of more affluent children.[6]

27

violence. Poor youngsters may be more likely to turn to drug dealing or extortion to gain money.

Availability of Guns

The startling proliferation of guns in the United States has had a negative effect on schools and school violence. Many sources state that there are more than 250 million guns in the United States, almost one for every citizen. One 1993 study revealed that a hundred thousand students carried guns to school nationwide.[7] Many students claim that they need a handgun in order to feel safe. A gun may give them feelings of power, strength, and self-righteous importance. There have been many reports of guns being involved in disputes over verbal insults or stealing lunch money or other minor disagreements. On the street young people have been killed for their sneakers or jackets. These problems, connected to the easy availability of handguns, often explode into violence and death.

It is easier in many communities to buy a gun than it is to pass a school exam. Most guns are initially borrowed, stolen, or retrieved from family members. Some researchers think that youngsters' interest in guns is spurred by parents who keep guns at home. Guns suggest control and power. They are seen as giving status to the owner. At times guns are carried for that image alone. Packing a gun seems to say to others, "I'm important. I'm strong. Don't bother me." If a person carries a gun, there is a possibility that he or she might use it. When that occurs, tragedy can result.

This issue of handguns is closely connected with

> In northeastern Kentucky in 1993, a seventeen-year-old honor student brought a .38 caliber gun to school and killed his English teacher and a janitor. He took his class hostage.[8]

issues mentioned earlier. Sophisticated weaponry, "designer" guns, and small firearms have been glorified in movies and television. Gangs and drug sellers stockpile small arsenals of weapons. These firearms are used to support the gang's status, strength, and willingness to hold their turf at all costs. Drive-by shootings display this power but endanger the lives of innocent people. Many drive-by shootings take place on or near school property. Normal sports rivalries and competition that occur between schools can escalate into a shooting incident.

Many Americans feel a sense of fear. They walk the streets, shop the malls, and attend school afraid that they will be robbed, beaten, or even murdered. They believe that they need to fight back against violence on a personal level. Karate courses, self-defense manuals, and personal safety devices such as Mace, pepper gas, whistles, and shriek alarms are being sold in growing numbers. This attitude is pervasive. Many students feel

Cheap, available handguns put all students at risk.

the same way. For some, carrying a gun is the strongest, most powerful form of personal defense they can obtain.

The problem for schools is that, just like pencils, calculators, and books, if students possess guns and bring them to school, they will be used. When that happens everyone is in danger.

Decline in Respect for Life and Authority

Some students kill or attack others over simple insults or disagreements. Afterward they show little regret. They display a sense of calm detachment. Guilt is an emotion that does not seem to exist in the modern, aggressive teenager. Many students do not see themselves as members of a school or the larger community. They look out only for themselves, their families, their gangs. This view of life encourages an "us versus them" attitude. These young people have been so desensitized to violence that after they engage in violent behavior they display few feelings of remorse or sorrow.

Even students who are eyewitnesses to acts of violence tend to report their accounts of the incident without feeling. Many young people describe muggings, brutal attacks, and even shootings in a bland, expressionless, matter-of-fact retelling that can be frightening. They seem more emotional about being interviewed by a camera crew from the local television station. The desensitization mentioned earlier is easily seen in these instances. The mean lives and negative

> In Beaumont, Texas, a high school football game was stopped when a player was wounded in a drive-by shooting. The game was rescheduled for the next day, but no fans were allowed to attend.
> In Richmond, Virginia, a student was shot in a high school parking lot during a Friday night basketball game.[9]

experiences of many young people leave them without sympathy. Their ability to feel shock and sadness at the tragedies of others is stunted. The only strong emotions that they do possess and display are anger and rage.

Schools and teenage society are dominated by popular social groups, or cliques. Some of these groups, both boys and girls, are made up of sarcastic, aggressive bullies. Teenagers often look up to classmates who have a bold, confrontational attitude. The individual who flaunts, mocks, or disdains the system gains status. Schools attempt to work with difficult students. Counseling and classes based on their academic levels are available. But those strategies do not always work.

Schools are set up to reward student achievements based on learning. They measure students through tests, reports, quizzes, and papers. The students who succeed according to these school values may win awards and honors, but they may also be insulted and ridiculed by aggressive classmates who are acting out. These dominating, often popular students do not value hard work, experience, and intelligence—characteristics of successful students. They do not respect people (such as teachers) because of their age, title, or education. Such students respect only money and those who make a lot of it. They make fun of teachers. Wit, sarcasm, strength, or cunning are considered more important than knowledge. The increase in such students' popularity is a problem for school order and safety, especially when other students follow their lead. All these factors lend themselves to a less than positive climate for education.

Handling Disruptive Students

In 1974, Federal Law 94-142 came into effect. This law stated that all children should be educated in the "least restrictive environment." This meant, in effect, that disabled students should be able to attend public school. Adjustments would have to be made to accommodate those students. A great change was set in motion, establishing many special education programs designed to aid students in obtaining an education and remaining in the public school system.

For most handicapped students this law has been a tremendously positive force. Students, from those with minor learning disabilities to Down's syndrome, have

> Twenty-five percent of students have more difficulty concentrating in class because of violence in their schools and twenty-one percent are less eager to speak up in class. Seventeen percent want to change schools or consider changing schools. Seven percent stay home from school or skip classes.[10]

been placed in mainstream school settings with appropriate adjustments. They are helped to learn and have done well.

The law also means that public schools must educate students who are classified as emotionally disturbed. This places heavy demands on schools. Resources are stretched thin. Students with severe behavioral and disciplinary problems due to emotional causes must be educated. Youngsters who in the past would not have gone to regular school because of their negative behavior are now attending mainstream schools. They receive special attention but usually attend some classes in the mainstream. Their behavior affects other students in the hallways, cafeteria, in special classes, and on the school bus. In the volatile mixture of the modern public school these students cause difficulties for staff and other students. Schools work hard to cope with the added burden of these students' special needs, but the work is difficult and success is sometimes limited.

Overall, the changes that have occurred in American society over the last decades are far-reaching and of great concern. Schools are simply reflections of society. Drug and alcohol abuse, media violence, families in stress and transition, poverty, guns, lack of respect, and the education of disruptive students are problems both for society and for schools. Schools do not exist in a vacuum. Difficulties in homes, neighborhoods, and towns are carried into schools along with the students who are forced to deal with such problems. As long as these issues are outstanding in the community, they will affect our schools as well.

3

School Campus or Prison Camp?

Americans want safe schools. Educators, parents, and citizens all agree on this fact. If a school is busy using its resources and energy fighting violence and crime, it cannot teach. A disruptive student takes away time and resources from the education of others. Various methods are used to counter the climate of fear in our schools. School administrators, supported by society and backed by the courts, are trying to make changes. The central question and debate is how far will schools be forced to go to ensure safety? When does the actual act of keeping a school safe become an act of disruption in itself?

Consider the following description:

- Each day thousands of young people pass through metal detectors to identify whether they are carrying weapons such as knives or guns. At some locations people can enter the building only if they have a security card. Some buildings use specially coded security locks. At a point inside, individuals are randomly chosen to submit to another check by an armed guard. This time a handheld metal detector is used.

- Closed-circuit television cameras monitor movement. The behavior of the crowd is watched carefully. Young people move from place to place and room to room. Passing time between rooms is closely checked. In many cases, youngsters have four minutes to move from one assigned location to another. Bathrooms are locked and anyone wishing to use a toilet must sign out a key from an adult in charge. They must sign back in when they return, redepositing the key. Bathrooms are monitored frequently by staff. Any vandalism, graffiti, or suspicion of smoking or other misbehavior is reported immediately. Reviewing bathroom sign-out sheets is part of the daily routine for staff.

- Two or three armed guards monitor various locations. The hallways, cafeteria, offices, and several classrooms are high-priority areas throughout the day. Guards are connected to the main office and other security personnel by walkie-talkie. Help may be needed at any given moment in a particular area. The guards' presence breaks up groups or crowds that congregate. Young people are herded to their next location.

- Outside the building another armed guard in a clearly marked police car patrols the large parking lots. The guard may at times walk the grounds of the building. Occasionally the guard drives through local streets and neighborhoods. Young people attempting to leave are detained by the guard. Their names are taken and turned in to facility authorities. License plate numbers are randomly recorded. Young people are closely monitored as they leave at the end of the day.

• When the facility closes for the day a series of safety measures are begun. Large metal cyclone fences are shut, internal security monitors and alarm systems are engaged. In some locations closed-circuit television systems come into play. In areas of high crime, armed personnel remain on patrol throughout the night.

Some of these scenes regularly take place in prisons and most international airports, but we are not describing such places. These scenes are the reality for some American high schools and their students. It is common to visit a school in this country in any large metropolitan area and see many of the forms of deterrence listed above. Most high schools across the United States have some of the forms of security mentioned above. Some actually have them all.

Child behaviorist Bill Steele of Detroit's Institute of Trauma and Loss in Children says, "There's no doubt that our violent society has eroded the security and safety of our schools and is creating an environment of fear, anxiety and trauma that is counterproductive to learning."[1]

"We're thrilled when we get news of a fistfight. It's a relief to know there are no weapons involved," says Gary Dell of the Wayne Westland School District in Michigan. Ten weapons offenders were expelled in Wayne Westland in 1994.[2]

Nathan Faris was a slightly overweight, brainy twelve-year-old who hated going to DeKalb Junior-Senior High School because of the constant teasing he received

Security systems, closed-circuit television cameras, and photo IDs have become as important as books and pencils.

there. He vowed revenge on his tormentors and one day brought in a .45-caliber automatic and twenty-four rounds of ammunition. In his first period social studies class, five shots were fired. Nathan and a classmate lay dead.[3]

Students can find ways to get around the strictest security measures. A handgun can be left in a paper bag on a windowsill. A clean walk through a metal detector and five minutes later the gun is picked up. Some types of firearms are made totally of plastic and are undetectable to metal detectors. Armed guards cannot be everywhere at once despite their best intentions. Students can easily pick up the routine of each guard and work around it. The bold, aggressive attitude on the part of some students cannot be controlled by high-profile guards and security systems. If one student is angry with another he or she will often attack despite prevention efforts by the school. Gangs have power and control in some communities and schools. Defiance of authority builds a reputation. If a gang member wants to gain prestige, what better place to do it than in school? An automatic audience of other students is in every hallway. A locked bathroom pushes students to deal drugs or to smoke in other locations in the school.

Well-behaved students are often concerned about or even insulted by the use of heavy-handed security. The vast majority of students attend school to get an education. The attention and worry caused by security checks and metal detectors distracts students from educational tasks. If a student is worried about a possible knifing or shooting, even when it is directed at some other student, it may be impossible to concentrate on schoolwork. In many cities students and teachers spend much energy designing programs to "win back" their schools. Antiviolence education, teaching and taking courses in conflict resolution, signing petitions, and arguing about and discussing the situation with administrators are all important, but time-consuming. That time could be directed toward education.

Robert Rubel, executive director of the National Alliance for Safe Schools (NASS) states, "If you get to a point where your school is fully secure, it's no longer a school—it's a prison."[4]

Even elementary schools are not immune to the need for security. Mohansic Elementary School in Yorktown Heights, New York, locks all doors except for the front door. All visitors are asked to stop in the main office, sign in, and wear buttons. Teachers are instructed to stop anyone who is not authorized to be at the school or is not wearing a button. Ann Perkowski, co-chairwoman of the Mohansic Parent-Teacher Association, had difficulty finding information about elementary school security. "We are not neurotics, not obsessive. We are not leading a crusade."[5] At Concord Road Elementary School in Ardsley, New York, all doors are locked and the school system pays an employee to sit in the front hall as a door monitor.[6]

Schools mirror society and the society of the United States is more aggressive than ever. The effort to create safe school environments is an attempt by concerned adults to gain control over an increasingly difficult and disturbing situation. Given the level of violence that occurs in some schools, old methods of discipline such as detentions and suspensions have proven inadequate.

Detentions after school, extra homework assignments, conferences with parents, and in-school or out-of-school suspensions generally work. They are effective disciplinary actions when used fairly and firmly with students who value school and their own education. Students who are motivated to succeed and have the desire to use their education as a starting point for later success tend to change their behavior when faced with disciplinary action.

School disciplinary measures are much more effective when supported by involved parents. In a 1989 Gallup Poll, teachers said that the biggest problem facing public schools is parental lack of interest and support.[7] More than one third of the teachers surveyed named this as the most critical problem for schools today. Some teachers added that they have "no backing from parents on discipline" and others charged that "parents don't help students realize the importance of preparing for the future." In some cases, parents side with their children, accusing school authorities of picking on, persecuting, or harassing their sons or daughters. They claim a "personality conflict" exists, attempting to shift equal or greater blame to the teacher or administrator.

Some schools and parents have made a difference in this area. Chicago-area schools have made improvements on many levels.[8] Farragut High School hired parents and community members as additional security personnel. Parker Elementary sponsored a Father's Day program and seventy-five fathers participated. Schools have established academic contests, mentors, monthly assemblies, career days, spelling bees, and a Kwanzaa program (for the African-American holiday in December).

Once a young person decides that school is not an important place, discipline rarely works. When youngsters think that school is designed to control and manipulate them, the types of disciplinary actions described above have little or no effect. Teens driven by the use or sale of drugs or alcohol or those with gang concerns and demands have little fear of school codes. Those caught in the cycle of school failure usually have no regard for the normal demands or requirements of school. In the midst of a knife fight, students don't think about the possibility of detention. Teachers are not equipped to step into the middle of such violence. The threat of a gun and its possible use eliminates any possible student interest in education. A detention or suspension becomes a joke.

Albert Shanker, president of the American Federation of Teachers, believes that students who disrupt classes should receive stiff penalties. He feels that schools need to do more to do away with violence and disorder.[9]

Schools, out of necessity, have needed to move to a higher level of discipline and control over student life within the walls of the school building. The first step was hiring security guards. This easily gave way to the presence of police at school. Plainclothes police saw that, in many cases, a uniform and gun added more authority and power to their presence. Each new level of aggressive deterrence has followed the past ones quickly. Each new technique has been an effort to retain or regain school safety.

Russell Tedesco is the director of security services for the Prince George's County, Maryland, school district. Serving twenty-two high schools and over one hundred eighty-six total sites, Prince George's County attempts to balance the difficult line between a secure environment and a prisonlike mentality.

The Prince George's County security plan is far-reaching.[10] Two Maryland state-commissioned special police officers are assigned to each high school as investigator/counselors. Most are experienced former police officers who have received training in dealing with youngsters and in conflict management and resolution. They are skilled in counseling techniques. Wearing plain clothes and unarmed, they work directly in the schools on all matters of violence, security, drugs, and crime. Although these officers possess powers of arrest, they are limited to on-campus crimes. If a student needs to be transported from a building because of an arrest, that is done by a county or municipal police officer and not an investigator/counselor.

In addition, there are thirty security assistants. These are non-police officers who work with disciplinary referrals. This removes the burden of discipline from school administrators so that they can focus on management and instruction in school. Ten additional field investigators are assigned to the elementary and middle schools. These investigators focus on violence, graffiti, school conflicts, and schoolgrounds problems. Four additional officers make up a rapid deployment team. They use two

Board of Education vehicles and can be sent to any school as needed at a moment's notice.

Twenty-four-hour-a-day security is also provided. Perimeter and motion alarms are monitored around the clock. All schools have security cameras. High schools and middle schools have handheld metal detectors. Locker searches and metal detection are used if authorities have strong and reliable information about possible crimes.

The entire $3 million security budget is supported and funded by the Board of Education. Tedesco feels that security is part of the fabric of Prince George's County schools, and states that he is "often included in general educational meetings and discussions."[11]

Prince George's County, Maryland, makes efforts to provide strong intervention and control while avoiding a military or prison atmosphere. These types of efforts are seen more often throughout the United States as the issue of safety takes center stage. Indianapolis employs a seventy-two-member school police force for its schools. The Indianapolis Board of Education passed a resolution to allow officers to carry firearms for patrols and emergency responses. Dade County, Florida, the fourth-largest school district in the nation, employs 131 officers for the 313,000-student school system.[12]

The use of metal detectors is a growing trend. One fourth of the nation's largest school districts use metal detectors. They are manufactured in two basic styles for schools. Handheld detectors can be used easily and quickly by school security personnel. They are light and transportable. An officer can stand at a doorway or move through a crowd with a handheld detector. Gateway detectors like the kind used in airports require students to walk through them. This type allows for more students to be scanned but is more permanent and difficult to move.

The legality of metal detectors has been an issue in recent years. Unlike use at an airport or bank, metal detectors at schools could be considered an invasion of privacy since students do not have the option not to attend. As of 1996 courts have upheld school use of detectors, but as they become more widely used, more cases will have to be decided in courtrooms.

Guidelines for use of metal detectors are created by boards of education. It is important that school districts have clearly written policies to support the use of any metal detection system. Justification for use, advance warning, and fairness are concepts that must be included in those policies. The overriding principle that courts have focused on in the use of metal detection and school searches is the idea of "reasonable suspicion." Although an administrator may have suspicions regarding a student carrying a weapon, he or she also needs to keep the "reasonable" aspect in mind.[13]

Many school systems use metal detectors on a random basis. New York City will often switch a battery of metal detectors from school to school in an effort to stop the carrying of guns onto school campuses. Students have become wary of this system and never know when they will be scanned for weapons. Weapon-carrying in schools has diminished.

Richard Silva, a security guard at Central High School in Bridgeport, Connecticut, states that the "carrying

Metal detectors prevent many weapons from being brought into schools, but students often find ways to "beat" the detection system.

of weapons has reduced dramatically since the use of metal detectors came in." At Central, the security officers stand at the door each day and randomly use the handheld detectors on individuals in no particular order. Students found with weapons are dealt with under the disciplinary code. According to Silva, even carrying common weapons such as knives has diminished greatly since use of the metal detectors.

The debate between school safety issues versus prisonlike settings is complicated and not easily resolved. There is no perfect method to guarantee school safety. That is part of the complexity of the problem. All agree that a safe school is important, but ideas of how to go about that differ greatly.

4

Prevention vs. Punishment

School officials, boards of education, and all citizens struggle to ensure the safety of children in school. The current attitude in American society is to be tough on crime. Courts, along with prisons, are expanding. Mandatory severe sentences for certain crimes have become popular. The death penalty is a fairly regular occurrence in some sections of the country.

This attitude is seen in schools as well. Serious disciplinary measures against students are more frequent. In Los Angeles during 1993 and 1994, when the city's new "zero tolerance" program began, 728 students were expelled for carrying guns or knives. That number of students is enough to fill a complete school—and it reflects student behavior in only one large city. Principals, teachers, and parents will no longer put up with violent and disruptive students.

The federal government is taking an active and

powerful role in forcing schools to expel students who carry weapons. In 1990, the U.S. Congress passed the Gun-Free School Zones Act. This law makes it a crime to possess a firearm within 1,000 feet of a public or private elementary or secondary school. Some students were prosecuted under this law. Challenges to the law have been brought by individuals. The Supreme Court has been called on to render a decision on its constitutionality.

Legislators are forging ahead in an effort to help schools control violence. In 1994, the U.S. Congress passed the Gun-Free Schools Act, which was signed into law by President Bill Clinton.[1] The law required all school boards that accept federal funds to adopt certain policies, including the automatic expulsion of weapons-carrying students for at least one year. Hailed by many people and school districts, this approach also raises legal questions and may be tested in court.

Prompted by societal and legislative pressures, many schools adopt "zero tolerance" policies. Zero tolerance means that any student involved in a violent offense at school with weapons or causing serious injury to another student has a mandatory recommendation for expulsion. Many school districts are using a strict zero tolerance policy with some degree of success. Most programs give the student the opportunity to apply for readmission. Some students have been expelled permanently. Numerous reports state that zero tolerance is powerful. When one or more students have been expelled, the number of these types of incidents then declines. This suggests that a strict, get-tough policy does result in less violent school behavior, especially those incidents involving firearms.

Chief of Police Alan Bragg heads the security division of the Spring Independent School District (SISD), in a suburban area of Houston, Texas. The problems of big-city Houston were spreading to suburban Spring, Texas. The people and school board of Spring decided they needed a police force just for the schools alone. Officials saw the changes in student behavior and the concerns over violence and crime that had arisen in Houston. They created the SISD police force. First commissioned in 1990, the SISD security division maintains a force of seventeen licensed Texas police officers. Two armed officers are assigned to each of the district's two high schools. Six patrol officers provide seven-day-a-week, twenty-four-hour-a-day service to all district facilities. Officers are equipped with clearly marked Ford LTD patrol cars. A dog trained in explosives and weapons recognition complements the force. SISD officers try to promote a friendly, helpful attitude to students. Officers are just as likely to respond to a flat tire or keys locked in a car as they are to serious disturbances.

Chief Bragg believes that SISD is committed to helping prevent crime in the schools and its support of the school police force goes a long way in achieving that goal. He expects that the force may expand in the years to come just as it has in the first few years of its existence.[2]

A clear Student Code of Conduct is contained in the Police SISD brochure. The responsibilities of parents, teachers, and administrators are described in the code, side by side with student responsibilities. Chief Bragg

Zero Tolerance

The zero tolerance stance is found in the Spring Independent School District brochure entitled "Creating a Secure Educational Environment." The document clearly states what SISD expects from students. It was written by the Board of Trustees and the school superintendent:

By ZERO TOLERANCE, we mean that we will be as strict as School Board Policy and state and federal laws allow (up to and including expulsion) if a student comes to school or a school event with a weapon. By a weapon, we mean a gun, whether it is loaded or unloaded; a knife, whether it is a pen knife, a pocket knife or a switchblade and whether it is pulled on someone or is simply in a pocket, backpack, locker or vehicle; and any other instrument that is used to injure or to threaten or to attempt to injure another person.

By ZERO TOLERANCE, we mean that we will bring to bear the full force of District policy and state law (up to and including expulsion) on any student who brings, sells, gives or uses drugs or alcohol at school or comes to a school event under the influence of drugs or alcohol. A student who has "only sipped" a drink, "only puffed" a marijuana roach or "only sampled" any type of drug will be dealt with firmly and decisively.

By ZERO TOLERANCE, we mean that we will remove a student from school immediately, and for as long as the law will permit (up to and including expulsion), when there is evidence that the student is involved in any type of gang or group that is intent on terrorizing anyone or ridiculing or mistreating anyone because of their race, their beliefs, the way they dress or a handicapping condition.[3]

states that the high-profile nature of the SISD police force is definitely a preventive measure directed at students who would commit violent or criminal acts. A measure of his belief is in their success: firearm confiscation fell from fifteen guns in the 1992–93 school year, to four guns in 1993–94, to only one gun in 1994–95. The combination of a positive, helpful attitude with a clear directive of no crime and zero tolerance has produced visible results in the SISD in Texas.

What about the negative aspects of zero tolerance? It can be a form of capital punishment for a youngster's educational life. Some expelled students never return to school. Their expulsion essentially forces them out of school. Uneducated, undertrained, and angry, these students have difficult times. They may be left on the streets with no intervention strategies in place. They may fall into the negative spiral of drugs or crime.

There is even some controversy as to the interpretation of zero tolerance. Students in rural areas often carry knives and jackknifes in their pockets. Are knives for cooking classes, home economics, or sewing allowed? What if a knife is part of a school display? A controversy did occur in a Midwestern state when a teenage girl was suspended from school for bringing in an artifact for a social studies report. That artifact was an African tribal knife.[4]

Many school districts hesitate to move too quickly to the zero tolerance concept. These districts believe that zero tolerance does little or nothing to help the individual. Most districts prefer to work within a framework that suspends a student for a certain number of days following an infraction. In many cases of suspension, the student meets with counselors or administrators upon his or her return to school. Some districts require offending students to view videotape programs on violence prevention. Others require a course or workshop. Students in some schools must join counseling groups. Administrators and boards of education have become increasingly aware of the rights of students to an education. They try to preserve this right while protecting the safety of all students.

Zero tolerance appeals to many citizens' sense of justice. They believe that some actions are so serious that the individual has lost the right to an education. The issue of firearms in schools is an area in which many adults join together in promoting a zero tolerance policy. This will continue to be a sensitive area, with supporters on both sides of the issue.

The question remains: If the United States as a nation moves to a greater use of zero tolerance, what becomes of the offending youngsters? In keeping schools safe, are town boards and administrators turning their backs on a number of students? Will these uneducated, angry teens eventually grow into destructive or noncontributing adults? Will they cost the state far more in terms of social resources for unemployment or even prison than they would have in school?

In Canada, zero tolerance is being used in certain districts. A thirteen-year-old who sliced another student's face with a box cutter was expelled and sent to a summer "boot camp" for impulse control. His reapplication to school was rejected. The board felt he was aloof and did not take part in therapy. The youngster was encouraged to apply to an alternative program called "Schools without Walls."[5] This school would be staffed with a support team including a psychiatrist, a teacher-tutor, and a youth worker. It would take place in the community: in libraries, community centers, and churches. Students could earn their way back into the regular school system.[6]

Many school systems believe that even the most disruptive or troubled individuals are owed a chance at an education. In these districts, teachers and staff feel that the last and best chance at changing the behavior and negative actions of problem students is by maintaining them in a school setting with appropriate intervention strategies.

One approach is to create "alternative school" programs. In these cases violent, disruptive students leave the regular school setting. They attend a separate school at a different location. The alternative school offers a smaller number of students. It also includes a better teacher-to-student ratio, a less formal campus and classroom setting, and intense individual or group counseling. Troubled youths have a chance to continue their academic studies. At the same time they are encouraged to work on their personal issues in a constructive, positive way. Alternative schools have the added bonus of removing these students from the regular school setting. The regular school consequently offers a safer climate for both teachers and students.

In many cases students return to their original school after a period of time at the alternative program. This

Confrontation occurs frequently in schools in the United States. A racial slur, an inappropriate glance, or a bump when passing in the hall often leads to conflict.

period may last from several months to a year or more. Some are even able to graduate. Unfortunately, alternative programs are expensive in a time when most communities are attempting to cut school costs.

Glenda Tinsley is a mother who turned her own son in to the police. Andy Tinsley first smoked marijuana at age nine. He always did poorly in school and was very aggressive. By the eighth grade he was sixteen years old. He fought with students and threatened teachers. He was arrested for breaking and entering. Finally, he harassed school authorities to the point of expulsion. Glenda called the police and had them arrest Andy for drug possession.

Andy spent time in juvenile court and is now attending an alternative school near his home in Louisville, Kentucky. He hopes his life will turn around.

Many advocates of schools and students believe that the best way to stop school violence is to work in a long-term preventive manner. The "primary prevention" concept states that with proper training and education young students can be socially prepared to handle the problems that they will encounter in life.

The first step in primary prevention is to uncover the reasons for violence. Next, it's important to teach young people the skills they need to know in order to prevent violent behavior. Recent research has found possible biological and genetic factors for these problems. Scientists state that concentrations of serotonin (a neurotransmitter) in spinal fluid is a predictor of violent behavior.[7] Additionally, *The New York Times* reported on a study that found violent offenders have higher levels of the male hormone testosterone.

Even allowing for these inborn characteristics, most authorities in the field believe that one of the main causes of aggressive and violent action on the part of children is that it is a learned behavior. Leonard Eron, professor of psychology at the University of Michigan, has studied aggression for forty years. He believes that from the very start children learn by observation.[8] Parents who yell, fight, or punish harshly or unfairly are likely to raise children who act the same way. Theory suggests that if aggressive behavior gets the desired result, most children will continue to act that way. Poverty, family stress, and media violence add to the difficult conditions faced by American families, but schools can make a major impact in the arena of primary prevention.

Consistency and fairness are extremely important qualities for youngsters to learn. Developmental psychologist Ronald Slaby states that the best strategies "systematically teach children alternative skills for solving problems, that challenge beliefs . . . about the glories of violence, and that teach thoughtful analysis to social problems rather than impulsive reactions."[9] Even aggressive play among children can be monitored and directed into more constructive actions.

Books, curricula, and classroom units teach how to negotiate, how to keep one's temper, and how to solve problems nonviolently. Preschoolers can learn these lessons as well as older students. In fact, many theorists feel that preschool is the most important place to start this type of instruction. Many youngsters attend nursery schools or Head Start programs. These children are at the perfect age for such lessons to make a significant impact. Study programs such as "Here's Looking At You, 2000" are designed to address important issues throughout the elementary school years.

The nationwide D.A.R.E. (Drug Abuse Resistance Education) program teaches young students refusal skills, problem-solving, and the negative effects of drugs and alcohol. Taught in the schools, often by youth officers from the local police department, this program expands the use of law enforcement officers as primary prevention advocates. The D.A.R.E. program is a high-profile, positive program that strives hard to achieve the goal of primary prevention with regard to substance abuse.

The concept of youth officers in schools, not only as representatives of police departments and law enforcement agencies, but as concerned community members focusing on helping students, is growing in popularity. Youth officers such as Rudy D'Ambrosio of Monroe, Connecticut, maintain a presence throughout the school district. In plain clothes when working in the middle or high school setting, Officer D'Ambrosio may wear his uniform for other duties or when working with younger children. Monroe, although a small rural town, has its share of teenage crime and school violence. Former president of the International Juvenile Officers Association, Officer D'Ambrosio believes that his fifteen-year relationship with the children is an invaluable asset in helping young people and preventing violence and crime wherever possible.

Many younger students know him simply as "Officer Rudy." Older students who are at high risk for becoming "problems" accompany Officer D'Ambrosio on visits to a federal prison. They see firsthand what the outcome of illegal violent behavior can be. D'Ambrosio knows students' older brothers and sisters, as well as parents. This helps to establish a foundation of support and rapport among students and school officials. Empowered to act with full powers of arrest if needed, Officer D'Ambrosio directs his energies at preventing problems before they occur, if at all possible.

The National Association of School Resource Officers (NASRO) offers an innovative program designed to train police officers who work in schools in

Officer Rudy D'Ambrosio confers with a school administrator.

any capacity. Their concept of a School Resource Officer (SRO) can be illustrated in their journal:

> The NASRO is a non-profit organization dedicated to the children of America. The School Resource Officers promote a better understanding of our laws, why they were enacted, and their benefits. They provide a visible and positive image for law enforcement. They serve as a confidential source of counseling to students concerning problems they face. They bring expertise into schools that will help young people make more positive choices in their lives and work to protect the school environment and maintain an atmosphere where teachers feel safe to teach and students feel safe enough to learn.[10]

59

In a letter inviting interested parties to the national convention for the NASRO, William Balkwill, president of NASRO, states, "The SRO Program is both a philosophy and a program that can work for agencies of all sizes. It requires innovative ideas, policies, and trust between a department and an involved school system."[11] The convention offered a course for school board personnel, as well as meetings for school board members, superintendents, principals, assistant principals, counselors, teachers, and parents. Training courses offered at the convention included Contemporary Issues and Violence, School Administration, SRO Basic Training Course, and T.E.A.M.—Techniques for Effective Aggression Management Training.

It is clear that schools must be safe. The best techniques to achieve that goal are now being fashioned. Experiments and new methods are being tried. A combination of strict rule enforcement, primary prevention programs, and a cooperative relationship between school and law enforcement officials seems the best path. Together they point in the direction that schools must move in order to ensure safety for all school members.

5

Models for Safety

Hundreds of school districts, towns, and cities are making headway against violence in their schools. Concerned individuals can make a difference. Classes, programs, clubs, and activities created to change school environments can and have been successful. Several outstanding efforts are described in this chapter.

States Institute School Change

Illinois. Dr. Leon Hendricks is the manager of the Safe Schools Project in Chicago. Working in over 550 schools serving 410,000 public school students, Chicago is testing and using a number of different programs. Dr. Hendricks sees children as "natural resources" that need to be saved, cherished, and used wisely. He believes that "teaching young people skills and giving them accurate and pertinent information will hold them strong for the future." He also feels that teaching students conflict resolution skills is an important strategy for growth. He encourages these skills in programs throughout the district.[1]

One example of a strong, positive program in Chicago is the use of a "mentoring" model, which connects young students with older students and adults. One elementary school was adopted by a group of community women. They worked with students as one-on-one tutors, mentors, and friends.

Rainbow House, a comprehensive social service agency in southwest Chicago, established "Choosing Non-Violence" (CNV).[2] CNV started as an abuse prevention minicourse for high school juniors and seniors. It then moved to primary grades and Head Start and child-care centers. CNV emphasized key concepts for children to learn:

- Violence can destroy people, places, and things.
- People have power to make choices about their actions.
- There are alternatives to violent response.

Violent acts have decreased in the schools where CNV has played a teaching role. The program continues as a concerted effort to choose nonviolence and instill that in schoolchildren.

Wisconsin. Many schools use mediation as a technique to solve difficulties between students. Mediation's appeal is that it helps youngsters to solve their own problems. When a dispute occurs, a student trained in mediation is called in. The mediator listens carefully to both sides. The mediator then helps to define positions and to offer insight, compromise, and solutions. A temporary working agreement is attempted. Contracts are utilized. Mediation is a workable, positive option for schools that is used successfully in Wisconsin and elsewhere.

Gilmore Middle School in Racine, Wisconsin, began mediation training in 1985.[3] Titled "Operation Safe," the purpose of the program was to make Gilmore a "safer, more pleasant place." First, teachers were trained at the Dispute Settlement Center of Racine County. Next, training was offered to the entire student body. After a committee screened volunteers, twenty-one students were trained in conflict-resolution techniques. Those students were then called in to mediate and help solve disputes between students. Each year the program has expanded. Students now look for mediation and contracts rather than fighting. A short list of recommendations for setting up a program in school mediation include:

- Joining a national association or contacting a professional mediator.

- Publicizing a mediation plan in assemblies, newsletters, and over the P.A. system.

- Forming an advisory council of teachers, students, counselors, administrators, and parents.

- Having adults trained.

- Purchasing or writing a curriculum for training students.

- Advertising for trainees and having them fill out an application.

- Selecting the trainees for student mediation.

- Training the student mediators.

- Starting the program (publicizing, distributing forms, organizing).

- Keeping the program going (holding monthly meetings, thanking by name the mediators who have worked recently, providing at-school services, giving frequent reports).

California. Huntington Beach High School in Huntington, California, tried a variety of techniques to improve the school environment.[4] The school had major difficulties with fights, violence, and students dropping out. In 1991, Huntington was considered a nonperforming school. However, in 1994 it was selected as a California Distinguished School. A new administration worked hard to change the school's atmosphere. The staff decided to focus on the goal of "personalization." Each and every student, especially those at risk, would be known and valued at Huntington.

The first step was to create an adopt-a-kid program. "Hot lists" were drawn up to identify at-risk students. Adult volunteers were matched with students. These adults acted as friends, confidants, mentors, and supporters. They met with students before school, during lunch, after school, and even during classes. Fifty-one percent of the students on the "hot list" improved their grades in each of the next two years.

Next, a "Most Improved Student Award" was established. These students were called out of class and presented with their award, in addition to a key chain, a certificate, and a letter for their parents. "Student of the Month" and "Athlete of the Month" awards were created.

Those students' names were placed on the school marquee. They were also named in the principal's newsletter, which is mailed home to all parents.

A student forum in the school conference room began meeting twice monthly, chaired by the vice principal. Students are able to discuss school policy and activities or voice any complaints. Students are being listened to and valued.

The principal began a yearlong green-ribbon campaign. This campaign promoted awareness of and expressed a no-tolerance position toward school violence. Students requested the green ribbons and wore them every Tuesday. The response was overwhelming. On Tuesdays, students wore green ribbons on shirts, hats, in their hair, and even on sneakers.

Following the success of the green-ribbon campaign, the principal organized a daylong school assembly. It included a panel with members from juvenile court and law enforcement agencies. Another panel member, one who had a dramatic effect, was a mother whose son had been killed by gang gunfire. Again, students were moved and involved.

Even the school day was changed. Block scheduling, a method in which teachers saw fewer students but for longer periods of time, increased student-teacher contact and relationships. The goal of personalization by Huntington Beach High School is being attained. Expulsion and suspension rates are down. Test scores are up. For the first time in a long while, teachers and students feel safe.

Horace Mann Middle School in East San Diego

made dramatic changes and a complete turnabout in school safety.[5] Horace Mann was a hotbed of conflicts and fighting. Mann has two thousand students, over thirty different languages, and a number of different races, religions, cultures, and nationalities.

The staff focused on several key concepts, such as the "child" and "person" are just as important as the "student" and school can be a safe haven. The overall environment must be positive. These beliefs began to move Horace Mann from a troubled building to a positive place of learning. School became a second home by creating year-round schooling. Students were never away from school for more than a couple of weeks. When needed, breakfast and lunch were given to students at school.

At Horace Mann, zero tolerance is strictly enforced. If a weapon is found on a student, that student is arrested, handcuffed by police, and removed. A school-wide discipline plan has been established. Teachers were trained in a specific theory using behavior management techniques. The school offers consistency in all classrooms and settings. Many types of rewards have been set up for positive behavior. The staff and administration constantly strive to create a positive school culture. They see young people as important individuals with unique needs and not just as numbers of students. Last year the California state attorney general chose Horace Mann as the site of a school-safety forum, not because of its past problems, but because of its current success.

Texas. Citizens of Abilene, Texas, focused on reducing the gang population in their city and the gang

Uniformed police personnel monitor school corridors. They are essential in hundreds of United States schools.

influence in their schools.[6] Most gang problems were centered near schools in impoverished areas. City officials, supported by citizens, decided on a strategy. Boys' and girls' club gymnasiums and youth centers were built next to elementary and middle schools in high-crime neighborhoods. The centers serve as school gymnasiums during the day. At night they are recreation facilities for youth.

Schools fought graffiti daily. Police took many measures to eliminate drug trafficking. Police increased their presence on the street and built rapport with residents. Private investors purchased buildings and attempted to build up depressed areas near the schools and centers. A 46 percent reduction in crime was reported in each area. Gang membership fell from 650 in 1988 to 75 by 1994.

Pennsylvania. The Safe Schools Project of the Pittsburgh Public Schools developed a multidisciplinary violence prevention coalition.[7] The school district, the Jewish Health-Care Foundation, the Western Psychiatric Institute and clinic, the Center for Injury Research and Control at the University of Pittsburgh, and the Boys and Girls Club of Western Pennsylvania formed an alliance. They wrote a "Blueprint for Violence Reduction."

Students began taking "violence reduction" classes. They learned that the violent hero is not glamorous. They realized that violence is only one reaction to conflict, and it is not the best choice. Next, they studied nonviolent problem-solving. Youngsters learned and practiced listening skills, summarizing, negotiating, and contract-making.

The "Blueprint for Violence Reduction" made recommendations:

- Violence prevention must be long-term.

- Prevention should focus on young children and at-risk youngsters.

- Prevention should include home, school, and community.

Studied by educators in other states and adapted as needed, the "Blueprint for Violence Reduction" has been used in Boston and other cities with positive results.

Philadelphia is attempting new methods to curb violence. School officials are being proactive rather than reactive to student safety needs. The School Safety and District Policy Committee, Alternative Programs For Offenders, and At-Risk Students Committee are all efforts at making a difference. They try to identify students and begin strategies to help create change before trouble begins.

Philadelphia serves one hundred ninety thousand students. The job of creating safe schools is monumental. Teachers, trying to work in the preventive mode, instruct students in how to be safe. Special sessions have been set up to work on more than just behaviors in school. Diverse topics are discussed. Students are given strategies. Ideas as simple as "don't wear gold jewelry to school" and "walk down well-traveled streets" are important. This instruction tries to combine school with community concerns. With this kind of instruction schools can be made safer.

Massachusetts. Elementary school students in Brookline, Massachusetts, learn strategies to cope with harassment. This program is called "Bully Proof."[8] Girls were being harassed on the playground. Boys bothered them with inappropriate words and comments. The boys would announce "Grab the Private Parts of Girls Week" or "Friday Flip Up Day" (pulling up girls' skirts on the playground). The girls complained and the administration decided something needed to be done.

Teachers, working with a Wellesley College researcher and expert on sexual harassment, began by asking kids to talk about behaviors they experienced or saw around school. The students wrote in journals and role-played some of the incidents. Girls shared their complaints with the class. Boys began to realize the problem and the girls' perspective. The behavior was no longer ignored. A "boys will be boys" excuse was not acceptable. Girls were clearly informed of their rights. They stood up more firmly and supported each other in stopping the boys. The behavior was not considered "fun" or "simple teasing" anymore. In Brookline, through direct instruction in classes, students developed strategies and refusal skills. They dealt more effectively with a problem. Early education proved, once again, to be an important factor for success.

Creating "Peaceable" Schools

In 1985, New York City Public Schools and the New York City Chapter of Education for Social Responsibility started to work together. The Resolving Conflict Creatively Program (RCCP) was created. Resolving differences is the cornerstone of this collaboration. It is an effort to teach children a "new way of fighting."[9] Since its beginning, RCCP has expanded beyond the scope of New York City. In the 1993–94 school year, one hundred twenty thousand students from three hundred schools across the country participated in the program. Cities as diverse as New York; New Orleans; Vista, California; South Orange/Maplewood, New Jersey; and Anchorage, Alaska, joined in.

RCCP aims to create a "peaceable school." The program educates for intergroup understanding, alternatives to violence, and creative conflict resolution. Teachers normally devote an average of seven class periods per month to conflict resolution. This instruction has a positive effect. Teachers note less physical violence in their classrooms. In addition, students have decreased their use of verbal put-downs, spontaneously used conflict resolution skills, and increased leadership skills and initiatives.[10]

"Stop the Violence, Save Our Children"

Reverend Jesse Jackson's wife heard a commotion outside and went out to investigate. There on her own street was a triple murder—three youths had been gunned down in the back of a car. Jackson had had enough. He called a rally to "Stop the Violence, Save Our Children!"[11] He called for a "victim-led revolution" to take back the streets and schools from the killers and drug dealers. He called youth violence "the premier issue of the civil rights movement today."

Jackson encourages the family, community, and school to band together. He wants to empower individuals to fight against the rise of crime, drugs, and violence in American cities and schools. Mentoring teams, church

71

involvement, and the active participation of community individuals and organizations is essential. "Taking back the streets" is a rallying cry for Jesse Jackson.

One program he had begun in the past was PUSH-EXCEL, a nationwide effort designed to get parents involved in their childrens' education.[12] In the early 1990s, Jackson began taking his crime crusade directly into high schools. He suggested that students report other classmates who carry guns and peddle drugs. "Turn them in!" Jackson exhorted. Sometimes he was met with derision. Young people stated that Jackson did not understand the conditions urban students lived with in the modern world. They said that they would be killed if they turned in their classmates. Jackson often countered with personal stories of the violence he had experienced early in life.

In July 1995, Jackson was the moderator at the National Education Association (NEA) convention for a presentation titled "Focus on Educational Change." Jackson reminded the nearly nine thousand delegates that "Parents want their children to be safe in schools."[13] National figures such as Reverend Jesse Jackson have continued to highlight education and safety in schools as a primary issue for America in the 1990s.

Sharing Data to Combat Violence

The National School Safety Center (NSSC) is a nationwide nonprofit organization. It offers resources to schools and individuals at a reasonable cost. It was established by the federal government and Pepperdine University during the Reagan administration in 1984.

The NSSC offers hundreds of pieces of information to individuals, school systems, and legislators. The NSSC helps combat problems of crime, drugs, and violence in schools so that educators are free to focus on their primary job: teaching our nation's children.

Items offered by NSSC include books, resource papers, films, videotapes, and display posters. *School Safety*, the NSSC news journal, is published three times a year. It is distributed to nearly fifty thousand school administrators, chief law enforcement officers, state and federal legislators, juvenile and family court judges, journalists, subscribers, and the governors, attorneys general, and school superintendents of all fifty states. Information is well researched and thorough. Completed by experts in the field, NSSC research offers understanding and advice for those who would like to be better informed. These documents also teach new strategies to aid in the fight against school violence. One area of emphasis by the NSSC is to find cooperative, positive solutions to school violence.

Areas that have been covered in depth in *School Safety* include weapons in school, security at athletic events, bullying, student searches, media violence, ethnoviolence, teacher victimization, discipline and corporal punishment, hiring the right people, and school arson.

In addition, the NSSC offers three-day leadership training workshops at various sites throughout the country. Schools with specific problems or special crises can call the NSSC for on-site technical assistance. A national clearinghouse like NSSC keeps information current and accurate and sends that information to the widest possible audience.

Creating Safe-Schools Legislation

The most important, centralized, and national-level directive to make schools less violent is the Safe Schools Act of 1994. This is part of the overall Goals 2000 legislation. It was signed into law by President Clinton in March 1994. The act provided funding of approximately $20 million in that year to create drug-free and violence-free schools by the year 2000.

Under the bill, school districts with high juvenile crime or homicide rates could apply for grants of up to $3 million lasting eighteen months. The money could be used for security equipment, hiring security personnel, studies, counseling, mentor programs, and awareness and prevention seminars. No more than one third of a school's grant could be used to purchase metal detectors. Forty-seven states met qualifications and participated on some level with the Goals 2000 Act in 1994.

The year 1995 proved a difficult one for education funding and safe-school legislation. A new Congress, seated in January 1995, took a hard look at the act. Attempting to cut the overall budget, the House of Representatives decided to cut nearly 50 percent of the funding for the Safe and Drug-Free School Program.[14] President Clinton used his first presidential veto to kill the bill less than twenty-four hours after it arrived on his desk in June 1995. Supporters and educators said that losing their Safe and Drug-Free Schools grants would cripple efforts to combat drugs and violence. The bill

President Bill Clinton signs Goals 2000 legislation, which will provide funding to create drug- and violence-free schools.

would have cut $236 million from the $482 million program.

President Clinton addressed supporters at a ceremony in the Rose Garden to honor ninety-eight schools for their efforts under the program. "There's a deficit in this country in the number of safe schools. There's an education deficit in the country. I cannot in good conscience sign a bill that cuts education . . . "[15]

In March 1996, the Senate voted 84 to 16 to restore $2.7 billion in cuts it had previously proposed. This includes $350 million for Goals 2000 and $400 million for Safe & Drug-Free Schools.[16] The House accepted most of the Senate's recommendations. Although not 100 percent of the requested funds were approved, Congress has accepted that safe schools are a priority.

6

Safe Health Environment

Schools need to be safe from handguns and violence. They must also be warm, clean, and free of germs. The toilets and faucets should work. The rooms must be well-lit. The air should be fresh, healthy, breathable. Graffiti should be nonexistent. Food should be nutritious. The building must be free of insects, rodents, and other vermin. Stairways should be safe. Elevators should work. Ceilings should be intact. Roofs shouldn't leak. Chemicals, dust, mold, and spores should not be present.

The average student spends over thirteen thousand hours in school from grades one through twelve. Parents would never consider sending their children to unhealthy factories for thousands of hours. Schools should be healthier than a typical factory, but they are not.

The concepts of health and safety go hand in hand. They are the very foundations on which schools are built. Worrying about guns and physical violence but

> Doris Rapp, M.D., reported the following case. An allergy-sensitive thirteen-year-old boy developed several medical complaints upon returning to school in September 1992. He began with nasal symptoms, a tight chest, and headaches. After a few weeks his ailments progressed to hives, itchy skin, flushed color, and muscle aches. Eventually, he also suffered from mood swings, nausea, cramps, and diarrhea. On weekends and vacations his symptoms would disappear. Finally, he received permission to attend a new school; he improved within a week after the change.[1]

neglecting the "wellness" of a school building is wrong. At the very least, schools must be environmentally free of health hazards and toxic concerns.

Concerns for all aspects of a child's learning need to be taken into account. A positive attitude on the part of staff and students is essential to a positive learning experience. When students feel that their basic needs are being taken care of, they are better equipped to lend their

Gray-green, spongy mold covered classroom desks, books, and walls at Stoughton Middle School, in Stoughton, Wisconsin. The mold problem was the result of shutting down the air-conditioning system over the extended three-month summer vacation. One science teacher, Tom Palmer, said it was the worst he had ever seen. "It smells in there," he stated. Fourteen new textbooks costing $37 each may have been ruined due to warping. "I don't even know if we could use them," Palmer said. The school district hired an environmental management consulting firm to conduct air-quality tests. Students and teachers remained at school while the investigation was underway.[2]

energies to the demands of school. The trust that a school is a germ-free, healthy building can not be taken for granted. Food, shelter, and safety are essential.

Many schools are falling apart. Broken windows, graffiti, and leaking roofs are only part of this dismal picture.

Buildings need to be clean, healthy, and safe for students. On average, students spend more than thirteen thousand hours in school during their lifetimes.

Heating systems function poorly or not at all. Students roast in one part of a building while others are forced to wear their coats to class. Walls and floors are damaged from leaks that have been poorly patched instead of completely repaired. Electrical systems are out of date, out of code, or do not work properly. Computer systems, when they can be purchased, sometimes cannot be hooked up due to inadequate wiring. Use of new technology is impossible. Computer on-line services connected to a modem often cannot be used because communication lines are inadequate and new ones cannot be installed.

Overcrowded conditions in many schools overtax

At the start of the 1993-94 school year, an "asbestos crisis" occurred in the New York City school system. It was discovered that previous asbestos tests had been flawed. The start of classes was delayed for more than one million students. Emergency efforts were made to re-inspect every school. Even by late September several facilities had not been reopened. Exposure to asbestos causes cancer of the lungs, esophagus, stomach, colon, and other organs.[3]

facilities to the breaking point. Tremendous wear and tear occurs to rugs, floors, walls, and desks. Asbestos cleanup is an ongoing industry. Schools are closed over vacations while old sources of asbestos are uncovered and removed. The safety precautions taken by firms that specialize in asbestos removal are shocking. They include sealing off all rooms and corridors, wearing special suits and breathing apparatus when removing asbestos, and using sensors to carefully monitor the air during removal.

Older schools suffer from allergy-causing dust and mold and other allergens. Ventilation systems are nonexistent, not hooked up, or not working. Many classrooms have no windows at all. Those rooms, designed to avoid distractions, or rooms that are pushed into use due to overcrowding, may provide little or no fresh air. The apparently simple issue of the proper heating and cooling of school buildings can have a major impact on students' health and ability to learn. Many schools, especially those in the northern half of the country, have no air-conditioning at all.

"Sick-building syndrome" means the existence of a less than healthy environment. A sick building presents living and working conditions that are unsafe, toxic, or health-damaging. Many schools suffer from sick-building syndrome. They contain lead, radon, asbestos, pest controls, formaldehyde, and substances that can cause severe allergies. Students are more susceptible today to the environmental hazards associated with schools than at any time in the past. Schools may ban smoking, but they often lag far behind in some "hidden" pollutants.

The federal government recognizes the importance of the environmental concerns of schools. Laws demanding

> School officials in Alexandria, Virginia, began an investigation of four main ventilation systems in June 1995 after one hundred forty students tested positive for tuberculosis. The Virginia State Health Department found that 8.6 percent of the one thousand six hundred nineteen students and staff at T. C. Williams High School were infected from exposure to the airborne tuberculosis bacteria.[4]

environmental codes have been passed. But the building and maintenance of most schools is controlled by local governments and boards. In October 1994, Environmental Protection Agency Administrator Carol Browner stated that "the government must take measures to protect children from toxins they come into contact with in their homes, backyards, schools and playgrounds."[5]

Children have special concerns that must be considered. A new medical diagnosis is titled ETI (Environmentally Triggered Illness).[6] If a child's body is unable to maintain a healthful balance due to environmental factors, he or she may suffer from ETI.

A boy named David suffered from Attention Deficit Hyperactivity Disorder (ADHD). He behaved terribly, throwing tantrums and defying authority at times. His parents discovered that he was extremely sensitive to odors and fragrances. They kept their home fragrance-free. The school was considerate of David's needs and helped to control pollutants. At one point though, his behavior had deteriorated. His mother went to the school and noticed a new computer table in the classroom. It had an obvious odor. The table was made of particleboard. This substance outgasses (puts out into the atmosphere) formaldehyde. The table was removed and David's outbursts disappeared.[7]

Symptoms of this illness might include headaches, asthma, nasal congestion, stomachaches, muscle and joint aches, and itchy rashes. Other less distinct, yet possible signs can include irritability, fatigue, spaciness, lack of enthusiasm,

Even school improvements, like a new carpet, can cause problems. Toxic chemical fumes emitted from new carpets and the glues used to cement them include toluene, xylene, benzene, and 4-phenylcyclohexane (4-PC). Rugs treated with pesticides, fungicides, and stain-resistant chemicals are even worse. Health problems associated with exposure to fumes from new carpets include eye, nose, and throat irritation; headaches; rashes; nausea; fatigue; respiratory problems; and asthma. Dr. Doris Rapp states: "From the environmental medical point of view, carpets should not be placed in schools . . . [the onset of] chronic health, memory, and mood problems trace directly to the time that new synthetic carpeting was installed."[8]

"just not feeling well," or apathy about performing tasks. The list of environmental factors is long and includes biological substances such as dusts, molds, pollens, danders, venoms, foods, and infectious organisms.

There are several reasons why children tend to be more susceptible to health issues:[9]

Body weight—Children are smaller and weigh less than adults. Contaminants enter their bodies more quickly and affect them more severely.

State of nutrition—Many children come to school without having eaten at all. Poor nutrition is rampant. Students lack essential nutrients and vitamins in their diets.

Immature immune system and immature nervous system—Children are not physically developed. Children's bodies are much less tolerant of infection and thus are more open to infection than adults.

Inability to deal with addictive exposures—Children are not able to fight off exposure to materials that may have addictive qualities.

On October 27, 1992, the Westchester County, New York, Department of Public Health closed down the Eastchester High School for three weeks, after students and staff complained of headaches, nausea, eye irritation, and respiratory problems. The school had been treated the day before with insecticides, including diazinon.[10]

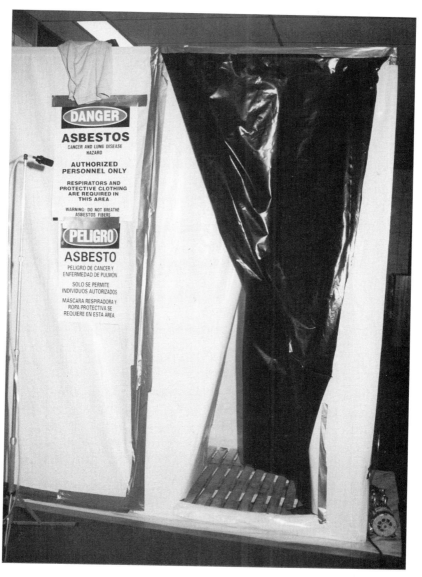

Health dangers are everywhere in old, decaying schools.

School contamination—Many schools are extremely old and contain a number of contaminants, from radon to asbestos to mold.

Frequent use of medications—Young people today take more medications and in larger doses than at any time in the past. Medication for allergies and asthma, medications that affect learning (such as Ritalin), and many over-the-counter medications are being administered every day to hundreds of thousands of youngsters.

Difficulty in understanding a child's complaints—Ambiguous, nonfocused complaints by children are often disregarded as "growing pains" or "trying to get out of work." Adults, in a desire to get their children off to school, sometimes miss the signals that may lead toward illness.

A report titled "School Facilities: Condition of America's Schools" was released by the U.S. General Accounting Office (GAO) in early 1995.[11] It was the first report on the physical conditions of America's schools in thirty years. The GAO estimates the price tag for repairing the nation's schools to be in the range of $112 billion.

The GAO states two major reasons for this dire situation. Over the last twenty years, most education money was spent for innovations and teacher salaries. Facilities were neglected. The second reason concerns the life span of school buildings. Buildings built around the turn of the century were expected to serve for fifty to one hundred years. Those erected during the construction boom of the 1960s and 1970s have a life span of approximately thirty years. Both sets of buildings are ending their life expectancies at the same time. Reconstruction and upkeep are now essential. The cost is astronomical.

School districts are attempting to fight back. In Detroit, where 53 of the school district's 294 buildings were built before 1920, school repair was estimated at $1.5 billion. In 1995, the school system successfully passed a $1.5 billion bond. Educators designed a "lesson plan" to teach adults in the city what they needed to know about the school system's needs. They were successful. The money will be used for repairs, renovations, compliance with fire and safety codes, accommodations for handicapped people, and electrical system upgrades so that computers can be installed.

States such as New York, Hawaii, California, Texas, Virginia, and Maryland have tried a different method. They lease school buildings, renting them from their owners for a set period of time. Leasing provides help for school systems that are working within strict, fixed budgets set each year. Yearly costs are kept down and large initial outlays of money are kept to a minimum. Leasing also tends to provide more "student seat" or capacity per dollar spent. Facilities tend to be more modern, and janitorial services and maintenance can be left to the owners of the building.

Another alternative for building use is the concept of "shared space." Schools are being built combined with day-care centers, recreation centers, libraries, government centers, or even office or residential complexes. These arrangements can save money and get better use out of shared facilities such as the gymnasium, pool, bathrooms, or cafeteria. The buildings are often brand-new, equipped with the latest and most modern conveniences.

Even the proper lighting of schools is called into question. Several studies show that students often suffer from "malillumination" and "sunlight starvation syndrome." Fluorescent lights, which are commonly used, are problematic. They flicker, hum, and glare. They offer a limited portion of the total spectrum of light. These limitations are so different from natural light that students have distorted writing and drawing as well as educational performance problems that are light-related.[12]

They have also been constructed under newer, more stringent building codes and meet higher standards for overall safety, accessibility, and health. The use of shared space has been tried in New York with success.

One other option is for schools to move to year-round schooling. Under this plan, more students are generally accommodated in a single school building. Split shifts for students, shortened days, staggered school sessions, periodic weeks off, and summer sessions all help to reduce overall cost-per-pupil. The need for capital spending for new buildings is lessened. More money is allotted within the budget for maintenance.

The major school areas of health concern in order of importance are:[13]

- Heating, cooling, and ventilation
- Pest control
- Cleaning products
- Chemicals
- Fragrances
- Site selection
- Lighting
- Remodeling the school building
- Floors
- Art supplies

Although most schools state that they are clean, there is obviously a major concern over whether school buildings are really safe in terms of health. Safety means safe from illness, cancer-causing substances, lead paint, and a number of other toxic substances. Schools must be healthy and clean.

"For too long, we have regarded schools as safe, clean places to work. But today, we know that the workers and the students . . . are subjected to safety and health hazards that threaten their lives."[14]

7

What Can Be Done

Make a personal commitment that handguns will not be part of anything that you do. A handgun's primary purpose is to kill. Resolve that you do not want any part of handguns. Do not feed the crowd mentality that accompanies handguns. They are not exciting. Reject the notion that firearms are dope, cool, sharp, or any other word that casts a positive or admiring light on guns.

Say No to Handguns in Your Life

Fourteen-year-old Mary Jo Mahler was on the school bus to Old Bridge High School in New Jersey one morning. Another girl pulled out a .25-caliber Beretta semiautomatic.

> The whole ride to school she was showing the gun to about eight kids in the back seat of the bus. She kept insisting it wasn't loaded. The bus parked in the school lot and a boy asked to see the gun. He moved

to the seat next to me, pointed the gun down between our feet and shot it.

The gun went off, but no one was hurt.[1]

If a friend boasts about having a gun or wants to show you one, decline and walk away. Don't lend your encouragement to weapons that have injured or killed thousands of students across the country. Start in your own life and in those closest to you: your family. Do your best to stay away from firearms, even when they are used in self-defense.

Become Involved in School

Most schools offer a wide variety of clubs and activities. A school that has an active student body is safer, more positive, and more fun. Many schools offer soccer, band, basketball, math club, industrial technology club, football, science club, chorus, art, track, service club, work on the school newspaper or yearbook, and a wide variety of other offerings. Join in and lend your interests and talents. Many students discover a lifelong interest or their profession in the activities they pursue. Young people who belong to clubs and commit themselves to activities encourage cooperation and teamwork. They are better suited for accomplishment later in life. Clubs, sports, and hobbies offer lasting pleasure and an association with others and with school.

Trust Others, Especially Adults, If You Can

Find someone who will listen to your problems, ideas, and concerns. Parents, teachers, other family members, neighbors, and counselors are all potential listeners. Tell

Make a personal commitment that handguns will not be a part of anything you do—especially at school.

them your story. Trusting and believing in someone who is older and more responsible will give you an outlet to relieve your fear, frustration, concerns, dreams, difficulties, and anger. Often their wisdom comes from years of experience and trial and error. They may be able to point you in a direction that will make life easier. Their advice may show you options and possibilities that you had not considered. Some adults may even be trained in problem-solving. At the very least you will feel better because someone has listened to you.

Turn In People Who Carry Firearms or Peddle Drugs

This controversial recommendation is important. It needs to be considered if the nation is to overcome the climate of fear and violence that has invaded many cities and schools. Do it anonymously by leaving a note for a teacher or administrator. Make a telephone call to a school counselor. Information in the hands of the correct people can make a difference.

Shebuel Jackson was a senior, a baseball star, and college bound. He died in the hallway at Mount Vernon High School from stab wounds. He may have been an innocent bystander. Shortly after, school officials installed a hot-line phone number. The high school's three thousand students were urged to use it to inform officials, anonymously if they wished, about fellow students carrying weapons to school or about other trouble.[2]

Think of your brother or sister at the playground.

95

What could happen to them if someone is carrying a gun? Will they be able to avoid the temptation of drugs?

Learn New Strategies to Deal with Conflict

Instead of fights, threats, "dissing" (showing general disrespect), and name-calling, find alternatives to violence.

One possible technique is to play the "Invisible Game," in which the victim makes the bully "invisible." The victim never responds to taunts and doesn't look at the bully. He or she avoids them in the hallways and even avoids eye contact completely. The attacker expects a response. Eventually, the bully will leave the victim alone. This technique can even be used by a quiet or shy person. The Invisible Game doesn't ask for the victim to fight back. It allows him or her to be strong in a passive way. Enroll in courses that educate you in such skills as problem-solving, mediation, or listening, all skills that can help you deal with difficult people.

Speak Strongly in a Nonprovocative Manner

This often works with troublemakers. In a calm voice ask the person, "Why do you like to pick on me?" State that you don't think it's fair. Counter accusations by being logical and clear. Show attackers that you are not afraid of them. Confront them in a clear logical voice. Don't make threats or accusations. Bring the issues out into the open. If the aggressor continues to be sarcastic or violent, stay calm and offer your view. This will often draw a crowd of people who are not on either side and may defend you. Eventually, teachers and school personnel will become aware of the situation and intervene. If they do not, simply turn and walk away.

Seek Support From Parents, Peers, and Teachers

You are not alone in confronting violence in your school. Ask your friends if they will stand by you in situations that are trouble. The old statement "in unity there is strength" is very true. Students do not want to feel alone or different from others. Part of the problem of school violence is that the good students are less organized than troublemakers and are reluctant to confront them. At some schools students hold rallies and daylong or weeklong observances designed to stop violence.[3] These rallies help to focus school-wide attention on the issue of violence. In New Jersey, the State Department of Education is encouraging and helping every school to develop a written code of conduct defining the rights and obligations, as well as the rewards and penalties, for acceptable and unacceptable behavior, both for students and parents.[4] Parents will be asked to sign an agreement to abide by the code of conduct.

Learn How to be Assertive Without Being Aggressive

Attempt to reason with others. Never react out of fear or anger. State your concerns, problems, issues, and feelings clearly. Do not be afraid to state your grievances openly.

The use of "I" statements can help in being more assertive. In this technique, individuals use a "sentence pattern" in stating how they feel. It follows this format: "I feel . . . because . . . " An example is "*I feel* angry *because* I can't get my work done when there's so much fooling around in this classroom," or "*I feel* afraid for myself and my sister *because* people are always stealing our money before school. I don't know what's going to happen next." Stating feelings clearly and directly without attacking others can be very effective in dealing with problems. "I" statements are powerful, clear statements of feelings.

Learn to Compromise and Negotiate

The classic win-win situation means that each party in a dispute gives up something in order to gain something. Listening to the other person is key. Hear other people out and allow them to speak. Try to understand their side. See if they have incorrect information. Try to answer questions like: "What are we arguing about? How can we solve this? What do we do next? Can we talk about this some more?" If difficulties are approached and resolved in this manner, all sides gain. The key ingredients are:

- Learn to give and take.
- Don't allow yourself to be upset during negotiations.
- Practice in small situations.

You will realize that a win-win negotiating style can be used anywhere at any time.

Students who commit violent crimes in schools are arrested there.

School safety and the need to make dramatic changes is of primary concern. Americans are trying to deal with the problems of making schools safe for their children. They believe in education and are currently talking about the issues of safe schools. Nationally syndicated talk shows place the agenda in millions of homes across the country. In July 1995, talk-show host Phil Donahue aired a segment on his show about "Schools and Guns." The invited guests included a boy who was expelled from his Pittsburgh school for carrying home a BB gun for a friend. A civil suit was begun to defend the boy's right to an education.

Another guest was a teacher from Maryland who was

99

shot in the chest by a student he knew. The teacher's injuries included five broken ribs and a punctured lung, diaphragm, liver, and gallbladder. The teacher sleeps only three or four hours a night, relives his experience, and is going through "emotional rehab." The convicted student received a twenty-year sentence that was reduced to five years. Audience members were shocked by the leniency of the sentence.

Hundreds of school systems have adopted programs designed to increase safety and decrease violence in their schools. These programs vary greatly in their focus and implementation. The U.S. Department of Justice and the Department of Health and Human Resources are evaluating various antiviolence programs. The findings will not be available for several years.

Chalk Hill Middle School in Monroe, Connecticut, created CHAMP, Chalk Hill Anger Management Program. The more than eight hundred students were exposed to a lesson on conflict resolution. Students received a list of helpful hints to avoid fights. Poster and essay contests were held. A special activity week began. Challenge events and volleyball tournaments were held. Assemblies were conducted by the principal, the superintendent of schools, and the first selectwoman (a town official). Students were asked to sign pledge cards that stated, "I give my word, to do my best to manage anger, to be fight free, and not be a fight promoter." A banner hangs from the school flag pole stating "Fight Free." It will not be flown on any day that a student is suspended from school for fighting.[5]

Many theorists agree to a core set of guidelines in creating a safe school environment:[6]

1. *Demand high expectations.* Sights set too low will not achieve desired results for safety or education. Respect, dignity, and responsibility should be clearly defined and demanded. Administrators should live by the standards they expect from students. Belief that all individuals can be at their best in school is the first step toward achieving that goal.

2. *Have a clear, defined set of rules.* Students need to understand those rules. Consequences for inappropriate behavior need to be fair. Student handbooks help to publicize and clarify that behavior.

3. *Parent involvement is essential.* Students are not free individuals acting alone, but are connected with families, neighborhoods, and friends. It is important that the school makes every attempt to involve the family in their child's education and school behavior.

4. *The teacher's role is key.* Teachers must present a caring "open ear." A sense that teachers are involved with students but at the same time demand certain behavior, goes a long way in making a building safe. Caring behavior from teachers translates into trust and respect from most students.

5. *The administrator's role is also important.* Administrators should exhibit a strong presence, establish a rapport with students, take quick, decisive action when needed, and administer justice fairly. When an administrator is able to display these traits, the possibility for creating a safe school climate exists.

6. *Stay one step ahead.* Anticipate problems before

they occur. Have contingency plans ready for possible problems. Try to keep up on the signs of the times among students: trends, popular activities, music, styles, slang, new types of entertainment, and fads.

7. *Try to promote positive school activities.* Students who are very busy generally have less time to get into trouble. Teams, activities, and clubs are great ways for students to be involved in a school. Students who do participate in school-sponsored functions are less likely to want to damage or destroy their school setting. Involved students are more motivated and do not have the desire to get into trouble.

8. *Respect community influences.* Consider the community in which the school exists. Outside problems and influences cannot be shut off as students enter the school door. At the same time positive influences should be encouraged. At the Multicultural Magnet School in Bridgeport, Connecticut, a festival is held on the day that celebrates Portugal's freedom. Respect for the cultural background of students can add greatly to a positive, caring school climate.

Dr. Leon Hendricks, Manager of the SAFE schools project in Chicago, states,

> No problem can withstand our concerted attack. The past has shown that when we put our minds and efforts to changing or addressing a problem we are successful. If other large cities join with Chicago, we can overcome this and other educational problems.

Marvin Cetron is president of Forecasting International. Margaret Gayle is a nationally recognized educational consultant. In their book, *Educational Renaissance*, they see reasons to be positive.

> In those rare instances where a courageous and determined school administration has set out to eliminate drugs and violence from its institution, it has generally managed to do the job. Simply providing students with an island of safety has proved to be enough to raise their academic performance and reduce drop-out rates dramatically, even when nothing else in their environment has changed. . . . In this respect, our schools should be much healthier and more productive places ten years from now.[7]

For more information on school safety, violence in schools, or any of the topics discussed in this book, you can refer to the Further Reading and Where to Get Help sections at the back of this book. Several of the organizations listed in Where to Get Help offer in-depth articles on specific topics. With research, support, and commitment, the United States can be successful in eliminating violence, health concerns, and fear from schools so that American students can learn in safety.

Where to Get Help

National Alliance for Safe Schools
Box 30177
Bethesda, MD 20842

National Association for Mediation in Education
205 Hampshire House
UMASS
Amherst, MA 01003
413-545-2462

National Center for Environmental Health Strategies
1100 Rural Avenue
Voorhees, New Jersey 08043
609-429-5358

National School Safety Center
4165 Thousand Oaks Boulevard, Suite 290
West Lake Village, CA 91362
805-373-9977

Resolving Conflict Creatively Program
Educators for Social Responsibility
23 Garden Street
Cambridge, MA 02138

Chapter Notes

Chapter 1

1. *Congressional Quarterly Weekly Report*, Section Notes, February 26, 1994, vol. 52, no. 13, p. 804.

2. Michael Sadowski, ed., and Randy Meyer, *School Library Journal*, August 1993, vol. 39, no. 8, p. 17.

3. *Jet*, vol. 85, no. 13, January, 31, 1994, pp. 26–28.

4. Barbara McClennan, *Detroit News*, NDOT Edition, September 11, 1994, p. 1A.

5. Jo Anna Natale, *The American School Board Journal*, March 1994, pp. 38, 39.

6. Eloise Salholz, with Barbara Kantrowitz, John McCormick, and bureau reports, *Newsweek*, March 9, 1992, vol. 119, no. 10, p. 30.

7. Denise M. Topolnicki, *Money*, June 1994, vol. 23, no. 6, p. 129.

8. Anne Lewis, *Education Digest*, February, 1994, vol. 59, p. 56.

9. Howard Snyder and Melissa Sickmond, *Juvenile Offenders and Victims: A National Report*, Pittsburgh, Pennsylvania Office of Juvenile Justice and Delinquency Prevention, 1995, p. 55.

10. Ronald Sullivan, *The New York Times*, Late Edition-Final, February 10, 1995, Sec: B, Metropolitan Desk, p. 4.

11. C. J. Farley, *Time*, Section: Chronicles, April 11, 1994, vol. 143, no.15, p. 19.

12. Ibid.

13. Barbara McClellan, *Detroit News*, September 11, 1994, p. A1.

14. Kathy Bolten, *Des Moines Register*, December 26, 1994, Main News, Edition: 3 Star, p. 1.

15. Kim Rose, *New York Newsday*, August 13, 1994, News section, city edition, p. A06.

16. John Marcus, *American School Board Journal*, April 1995, p. 1.

Chapter 2

1. Thomas Pierre, *Washington Post*, December 13, 1994, Final Edition, Section A, p. A1.

2. Kathy Bolten, *Des Moines Register*, December 26, 1994, Main News, Edition: 3 Star, p. 1.

3. Donald C. Orlich, *Education Digest*, March, 1994, vol. 59, no. 7, pp. 4–6.

4. Howard Snyder and Melissa Sickmond, *Juvenile Offenders and Victims: A National Report*, Pittsburgh, Pennsylvania, Office of Juvenile Justice and Delinquency Prevention, 1995, p. 37.

5. Jo Anna Natale, *American School Board Journal*, March, 1994, pp. 34, 38, 39.

6. Donald Orlich, *Education Digest*, March, 1994, vol. 59, no. 7, pp. 4–6.

7. Barbara McClellan, *Detroit News*, September 11, 1994, Section: News, p. 1A.

8. Debra Ann Vance, *Kentucky Post*, September 15, 1994, Section: News, Edition: Kentucky, p. 1K.

9. Maggie Reichers, *American School Board Journal*, June 1995, p. 33.

10. *USA Today Magazine*, August 1995, vol. 124, no. 2603, p. 9.

Chapter 3

1. Barbara McClellan, *Detroit News*, September 11, 1994, Section: News, p. 1A.

2. Ibid.

3. Stuart Greenbaum, *Set Straight On Bullies* (Malibu, Calif.: National School Safety Center, 1989), p. 9.

4. Ibid.

5. Michael J. Sadowski, ed., and Randy Meyer, *School Library Journal*, August 1993, vol. 93, no. 8, p. 17.

6. Roberta Hershenson, *The New York Times*, December 11, 1994, Sec. 13WC, Late Edition-Final, Westchester Weekly Desk, p. 1.

7. Greenbaum, pp. 62–63.

8. Debra Williams, "Security Efforts Cut Chicago School Violence," *The Education Digest*, November 1995, vol. 61, no. 3, pp. 18–21.

9. Albert Shanker, *National Review*, February 7, 1994, vol. 46, no. 2, p. 22.

10. Telephone interview with Russell Tedesco, July 11, 1995.

11. Ibid.

12. Maggie Reichers, *American School Board Journal*, June 1995, p. 34.

13. Joseph M. Wilson and Perry A. Zirkel, *American School Board Journal*, January 1994, pp. 32–34.

Chapter 4

1. Maggie Reichers, *American School Board Journal*, June 1995, pp. 32–38.

2. Kerry L. Brusky, *Houston Chronicle*, This week section, January 15, 1994, pp. 1, 4.

3. Alan Bragg and Gordon M. Anderson, Spring Independent School District Brochure, *Creating a Secure Educational Environment*, Houston, Texas, 1995.

4. Reichers, p. 38.

5. Stan Josey, *Toronto Star*, September 22, 1994, Section: Scarborough, Edition: Final, p. SD3.

6. Ibid.

7. Nancy Wartik, *McCalls*, April 1994, pp. 98, 103.

8. Jo Anna Natale, *American School Board Journal*, March 1994, pp. 33–40.

9. Ibid.

10. William Balkwill, *NASRO Journal*, Autumn 1994, p. 2.

11. William Balkwill, National Association of School Resource Officers Brochure, Fifth Annual Conference, Sarasota, Florida.

Chapter 5

1. Telephone interview with Dr. Leon Hendricks, June 27, 1995.

2. Ann Parry, *Education Digest*, January 1994, vol. 59, no. 5, p. 42.

3. Suzanne Miller, *Education Digest*, November 1993, vol. 59, no. 3, p.13.

4. Rebecca Shore, *Education Leadership*, February 1995, pp. 76–78.

5. *Middle Years*, September–October 1994, pp. 37–39.

6. Edwin J. Delattre, *American School Board Journal*, July 1994, pp. 15–18.

7. Deborah Prothrow-Stith, *Education Digest*, November 1994, pp. 30–34.

8. Melissa Etlin, *NEA Today*, April 1995.

9. Linda Lantieri, *Education Digest*, April 1995, pp.14–17.

10. Ibid.

11. Paul Glastria and Jeannye Thornton, *U.S. News & World Report*, January 17, 1994, vol. 116, no. 2, p. 38.

12. Ibid.

13. Ann Bradley, *Education Week*, July 12, 1995, vol. 14, p. 10.

14. Richard Riley, U.S. Newswire Corp., March 16, 1995, (Statement by education secretary Richard Riley).

15. Robert C. Johnston and Adrienne Coles, *Education Week*, June 10, 1995.

16. Braden Goetz, Scott Barstow, and Patty Farrell, American Counseling Association, Government Relations Report, April 1996, p. 1.

Chapter 6

1. Norma L. Miller, Ed.D., *The Healthy School Handbook* (Washington, D.C.: NEA Professional Library, June 1995), p. 27.

2. *Duluth News-Tribune*, August 30, 1995. Internet site: http://www.Irp.com/Education/newed4.htm.

3. Ibid., p. 171.

4. *Indoor Air Review*, August 1995. Internet site: http://www.safeschools.org/

5. Vicki Allen, "U.S. Fails To Protect Kids From Carcinogens," *Reuters*, October 24, 1994.

6. Miller, p. 51.

7. Ibid., p. 129.

8. Ibid., p. 182.

9. Ibid., pp. 39–48.

10. Ibid., p. 246.

11. John Marcus, *American School Board Journal*, April 1995, pp. 37–38.

12. Miller, pp. 196–198.

13. Ibid., p. 64.

14. Thomas Y. Hobart, president of the New York State United Teachers. Internet site: http://www.safeschools.org/

Chapter 7

1. Karla Dauler, *The New York Times*, November 27, 1994, Sec. 13 NJ, Late Edition Final, New Jersey Weekly Desk, p. 6.

2. Elsa Brenner, *The New York Times*, December 11, 1994, Sec. 13WC, Late Edition Final-Westchester Weekly Desk, p. 1.

3. Stuart Greenbaum, *Set Straight On Bullies* (Malibu, Calif.: National School Safety Center, 1984), p. 69.

4. Dauler, p. 6.

5. The information on the CHAMP program was found in the Spring 1996 Chalk Hill Middle School parent newsletter. CHAMP was created by a committee of teachers and school staff.

6. Becky Meyer Monhardt, John Tillotson, and Peter Veronesi, *American School Board Journal*, February 1995, pp. 32–34.

7. Marvin Cetron and Margaret Gayle, *Educational Renaissance: Our Schools at the Turn of the Twenty-First Century*, (New York: St. Martin's Press, 1991), p. 216.

Further Reading

Blauvelt, Peter. *Effective Strategies for School Security*. Reston, Va.: National Association of Secondary School Principals, 1981.

Cetron, Marvin, and Margaret Gayle. *Educational Renaissance: Our Schools at the Turn of the Twenty-First Century*. New York: St. Martin's Press, 1991.

Goldstein, Arnold. *School Violence*. Englewood Cliffs, N.J.: Prentice Hall, 1984.

Shultz, Edward W. *Child Stress and the School Environment*. New York: Human Sciences Press, 1983.

Index